Of Salt and Song

Of Salt and Song

Poems by

Brooke Lehmann

© 2025 Brooke Lehmann. All rights reserved.
This material may not be reproduced in any form, published,
reprinted, recorded, performed, broadcast,
rewritten, or redistributed without
the explicit permission of Brooke Lehmann.
All such actions are strictly prohibited by law.

Cover design by Shay Culligan
Cover image by Martin Baron
Author photo by Judah Townsend

ISBN: 978-1-63980-720-8
Library of Congress Control Number: 2025936247

Kelsay Books
502 South 1040 East, A-119
American Fork, Utah 84003
Kelsaybooks.com

For Justin

It was only salt before I met you

For Kevin Davis

Who helped me find the courage to write this song

Acknowledgments

Many thanks to the following journals and magazines for previously publishing and awarding the following poems within this collection:

Black Fork Review: "Early Mornings with My Father"
Breakwater Review: "Her Thoughts as She Looked Back"
Nixes Mate: "Lot's Nameless Wife Takes Inventory"
Palette Poetry: "Aftermath" a long-list finalist for 2022 Sappho
    Prize for Women Poets
Pedestal Magazine: "To the Woman in the Salt"
Pinesong: "Thanksgiving Psalm" which was awarded 1st place in
    the Charles Edward Eaton contest
Poet Lore: "Birthday Elegy"
Streetlight Magazine: "Bullfrogs"
Tar River Poetry: "Tent Revivals"

Also, thank you to *Tusculum Review* for awarding my chapbook *Pillar of Exquisite Sorrows* which contains several poems from this manuscript a finalist in the 2023 Chapbook Prize.

I am eternally grateful to my beloved late mentor, Dannye Romine Powell, for the earliest notes on these poems and whose tender care shaped the forming of this collection. Your life and legacy continue through your voice, a fierce and salty wisdom that guided these pages. You saw talent in me when I was at my lowest. Thank you for believing in me and this manuscript. I was honored to know and call you a dear friend.

Thank you to my mentor Jessica Jacobs whose own writing had her exploring the book of Genesis while I was beginning to form the persona behind these poems. I am grateful for your astute editor's eye and encouragement on writing this manuscript. You pushed me to go deeper, and I am grateful for your generous and motivating-though-at-times-tough coaching—your skillful fire that sharpened my poetry.

I also extend many thanks to Kathie Collins alongside Dannye for the Charlotte Lit Poetry Chapbook Lab where this manuscript emerged. You helped me find my poetry community and warmly invited me to stay. Thank you also to the members of the Charlotte Lit Poetry Chapbook Lab for your generous feedback on my poems.

Thank you to my monthly poetry group of Joanne Durham and Duncan Smith who became beacons of hope during the pandemic and helped me find my way back to NC and to writing. You are my poetry champions, and I am forever grateful for the chance NC Writer's Network class where we first met. You have both made me a finer poet and person. You've added so much flavor, craft and laughter to my life.

Thank you to my other monthly poetry group that met during the making of this manuscript: Cindy Buchanan, Bill Hollands, Patricia Joslin, Paula Stenberg, Seth Rosenbloom, Kim Kralowec, and Judy Aks. You have all become tremendous supporters and good poetry companions. It's been wonderful to have your support these last five years.

Thank you to Lindsay Bridges of Charlotte Center for Mindfulness whose friendship and steadfast belief in poetry as a spiritual practice anchored me during the revision of these poems—and to the community who reminded me that silence—at least for me—is the beginning of almost every poem.

Thank you to Chen Chen who provided me inspiration on this manuscript and one of the poems in the collection. I am grateful to have spent time with you in Charlotte during your Poetry Nightclub event and consider you a generous teacher and poet. Holding these poetry roses you have gifted me closely.

Thank you to Kelsay Books for selecting my manuscript and handling it with care.

Thank you to Sharon Kugelmass who is one of my earliest writer friends and has become family to me. Thank you for celebrating me and Justin, and being such a good friend and neighbor—especially at times when I succumb to despair, and you gently nudge me to go write a poem.

Thank you to all my wonderful friends and community who encouraged me while writing and sending out my manuscript: Drew & Christyn, Shannon, Stephanie, Sophia, Brad, Louanne,

Joel, Carrie, Dia, Deepti, Jess and Danielle. I am grateful for you all and sending you much love.

Thank you to Kevin Davis whose trauma expertise and care as my therapist all these years have shaped me as a woman and a poet. This book would not have been possible without your healing hands and heart. You midwifed me into a woman who has reclaimed her voice, sexuality, and body. I am eternally grateful for your guidance. I would not be here today, nor would this book exist, without your essential work. Meeting and working with you has been one of the greatest blessings of my life. You led me back to my pen, my art. I am eternally grateful.

Thank you lastly to my husband, Justin Lehmann. Your steadfast love and support all of these years have been my bedrock. You showed me unconditional love during a time when everything felt dark, and I became shadow. You tenderly walked this path with me and encouraged me to keep writing and working on my poetry craft. You are my biggest fan (which so many good friends remind me). Your love is woven throughout this collection and the fabric of my life. I always felt the greatest story I could ever write was ours. Thank you.

Contents

I don't remember the reception except waltzing with you to Norah Jones.	15
In the beginning there was desire	16
Genesis	17
First Time	18
Lead Actress	19
The First Flashback	21
Silver Irises	22
Tent Revivals	23
Bullfrogs	25
To the Woman in the Salt	26
Incantation	27
Aftermath	29
Father Taunting Her with Psalms	30
The Summer the Flashbacks Begin	31
It's comin' up a cloud	33
Shapeshifter	34
Supercilious Man Calling Himself Angel	35
After Sodom There Was the Cave	36
You Asked Me About My Mother	37
I Dream of the Orca Carrying Her Dead Calf for 17 Days	38
Love Poem for the Year After My Hip Surgery	39
Lot's Nameless Wife Takes Inventory	41
My Thoughts as I Look Back	42
Birthday Elegy	43
A Queen Resurfaces	45
Spring Collection	46
A Word She Taught Me Called Pleasure	47
October	48
Equanimity	49
Castle Elementary in Southern Indiana Asks Its Third Graders to Sell Earth Day T-Shirts	50
Prayer	51

Horses & Roses	52
Coda	53
Thanksgiving Psalm	54
Early Mornings with My Father	55
Christmas Eve	56
He Asks Me Why I Love Winter	57
After Talking to Poet Chen Chen About Teaching a Class on Happy Poems	59
The Nestling Near Your Magnolia Tree	60
Ambivalent Selkie Finds Joy	61
Summer Communion	62
Update on Lot's Wife	63
I Imagine Being a Worm	64
Resentment	65
Duplex for the Waiting	66
Andante	67
Broken Chords	68
Legacy	69
Notes	71

I don't remember the reception except waltzing with you to Norah Jones.

With each box step, my arms carriage
to yours, leading me forward
and backward. One. Two. Three.

repeating in my head. It will be years
before you know how adept I am
at keeping count. *Come Away with Me*

is the only lyric I remember, along
with the soft piano and lights strung
above us. We must have eaten strawberry

cake and greeted our guests, but all
I remember, you spinning me,
my French-tip nails on your shoulder.

Later, you undress me out of the beaded
gown, tassel, and unpin my Rapunzel hair.
Afterward, we sleep deeply. I don't

tell you about the stone I carry
into our marriage. Years pass.
But there is a grace in forgetting,
at least for a while.

In the beginning there was desire

stone and red, a circle
of early mornings, steady-dark
and bloom shade. Dew drops
and cardinals singing
at dawn. There was a garden
before I knew sorrow—though, it doesn't
take anyone very long. So, I drew the edges
of my life with a ruler. Let it be
straight and narrow. Let it be kept
tidy and free of thorn and thistle.
Bark and rock. Might as well root-up
the roses, too. I've built a fortress
of triangles over my heart
where the scarlet bird of my chest
once lived. Now, I find myself centered,
red and stone in the dark and early
mornings tending to sorrow's song,
hours of the minor keys.

Genesis

My grandmother told me
as she braided my honeycomb
hair, in the beginning
of time, those early years—
It was just breath
steaming above water, dark
and formless. God hovering
like a hummingbird over
a sun-charmed lake. Before
stars or earth formed, or words
to describe black of night. Before
subjects and verbs. Or objects—
Mothers and Fathers. Daughters.
Before Genesis, its fire and salt.
There was an aching void,
a voice asked to create
and keep extending—like a line,
one that jumps out from itself.
Before my father's desire
it was pure imagination, *Light
Bright* and *Lucky Charm*
marshmallows. Dying eggs
in vinegar. Easter bonnets,
and spring kites. Piano recitals,
honeysuckle strung between
my gapped teeth, bare feet
in the creek near our house.

First Time

We walk through Kensington Garden
near the Peter Pan statue. Blue star
and crocuses make it feel like spring
break. I'm surprised my parents allowed me
on this senior trip. I've never been
anywhere besides a Florida beach or state
where distant family lives. Where I live,
Drive Your Tractor to School Day. That evening
your mother, one of our chaperones, realizes
her son now loves someone more than her,
and she is angry with us. We leave anyway
and stroll through the garden unaware
of anyone else. There is a *Teen Miss USA*
in our group, but your eyes only follow me
in my thin glasses and lavender windbreaker. We stay
out until there are nightingales and train whistles.
I sip my first Starbucks mocha. I've not given over
my body to you yet. My grandmother didn't raise
me to be a fool. I wasn't going to have a baby
before the chance to leave town—every teenage girl
at my church became pregnant before graduation
except me—a lover's touch transcends rules. I want you,
and now I know I love you. So, I open like a magnolia
cup unfolding in hunter green leaf and branch.
Tender, you ask if it hurts. And afterward, wonder why
there isn't blood. I lay silent in your arms and dark.

Lead Actress

(with a phrase after C.D. Wright)

Just behind the ice-blue curtain, you turn
toward the morning sun brightening
your face, the pearl and lace

of your wedding dress. The satin robe
wraps your bare legs, and the pencil-jab
lead still scars your knee, forever
etched in your skin.

From here, you look like a sculpture
stripped down, a bikini wax.
Near you, a doll and bridesmaids
sleep, gathered like blind puppies.

Rice packets pile next to fuchsia ribbon,
lined-up matching heels.

Now, you're alone.

A knock, but this time
you keep the door locked—
the roped vein in your neck
says only that
whatever your father's next
command is, you will not fulfill it.

See how bravely you turn, the deliberate
retreat into your own stillness, your rouge
cheeks burning in the mirror.

Before today, what sorrow
did you veil? I see your blue
shadows *casting deep shade,* irises
unraveling at your chest as you exit
this scene.

The First Flashback

I sliced daydreams on summer's lush cutting
board, tomatoes and basil, fresh mozzarella.

When the paring knife nicked my vein, blood
stung, and I remembered their faces,

beautiful and awful light blinded me
as thunder rolled and lightning flashed.

Supercilious men knocking at my door,
calling themselves angels.

"I need you to be still. This won't hurt."
as one touched, started at my collarbone.

There was a coldness to their voices,
earnest, but no sincerity
like when they preached—

familiar sights and sounds,
acorns snapping the ground
against hard rain.

Afterward, blueberries smashed
like small drops of blood
over the wet grass—

the stench of petrichor, my ears ringing.

Silver Irises

shimmered on my bedroom walls,
tear-stained, almost looked like weeping
angels—my head drooping under a star-quilted
blanket my grandmother stitched, counting
to a thousand each time he visited my room,
tawny nightlight glow, *Precious Moments*
clock ticking.

Tent Revivals

They start around seven when
the clouds are dusty roses
in the darkening sky. Crickets

chirp near the dull river
as my dress drapes heavy
on sunburnt skin. Tarry long

enough, *holy ghost* may bless
my tongue that would rather
be kissing the tan boy

with caramel eyes who whispers
that I am smart in English class.
Boy who doesn't know I spend

most evenings here,
and I am tired most days
when he holds my hand and asks

why I don't talk about
my family. He doesn't know
about these nights when loud

sermons simmer praise, as the dark
widens the preacher's voice raging
hellfire, I want to grab

a tambourine and flee
like gypsy Esmerelda I read
about in books. But my

mother makes me clap
and sing, stomp feet. Women
don beehive updos and shout

in tongues of fire around sparse
pews. Pray midnight weary when
I would rather read Jane Eyre

in dim light or sing lullabies to sleep
and dream about this beautiful
boy. Afterward, I avoid friends

and joy. Forget my father's reaching
hand which grazed my chest
during the altar call, my mother's

scolding me for wearing a loose
shirt as other the congregants
crane necks, look away. At school,

the boy wonders why I don't
answer his phone calls. Why I
don't speak anymore of beauty,

care to hear about his basketball
games, why I don't want to watch
soft blinking light of fireflies—

why my tremulous voice trails
off. My life is obedience,
my silence, all that's required.

Bullfrogs

Always in discord, they are
summer's yellow-throated singers,

so deep in distress, I cannot tell
if the voice is mine or theirs

cannot even tell if it is fright
or sorrow, the pained thrum

which gives to a humid night
echoes in the eardrum,

a reverb as haunting as
an owl or one's racing heart,

which lingers when they sleep
during the panting heat of day

while the moon seeps silent
under the bright horizon

what remains is close to sweat
and salty skin, a dizzy reminder

of hidden pasts, sounds
of the South and my fear.

To the Woman in the Salt

Woman of your own armored body,
stone of your heavy burdens.
If I could, I would give you water
from my hands and watch it dissolve

your salt. Your thirsty lips pressed on my palm
as if the heat of your mouth were the warmth
of morning—where a stag rests in the soft
grass until the fog begins to lift, waits
for light at the forest edge—

I know you miss daylight and walks
with your immoveable legs and tremors—
and the word *disability,* its five hard
syllables, a knuckled fist at your throat—
at night when you can't sleep, the blades
of the fan spin like dancing Sufis offering

prayers. I want to see you wake,
shaking the salt from your lids
as you open your eyes and taste
the ripe figs bruising dry ground,

ready, like us, to shed their skin.

Incantation

—after Mary Szybist

Over and over in the darkness I tarried
and fell on my knees repenting,
asked for you to rapture me

away from church and slick
haired preachers, asked for tongues
of angels to bless my prayers.

I waited for you to descend
but your flame never came
to the breath-steamed window,

my small hands writhing in silence—
waiting for the sky to brighten, a cloud
to lift and hear your wind. I looked

for you in the reflection of water
on the edge of the naked branch,
pearls after the storm. I waited

for you to rescue me like a beloved
daughter or friend. Now, I know
you're the apparition that passes

through my hours silently, dappled
prism on a wall, a broken blue
robin shell—loose blossom

brushing my skin in the cool
air. *Holy ghost,* you're not
savior or giver of miracles,

only muted witness, invisible
one who sees suffering
in those murky watercolors

dripping from all our eyes—

Aftermath

—after Anselm Kiefer's "Lot's Wife"

The last thing I heard, an owl hoot from the oak trees
behind our house. Then a hummingbird flutter, its ruby

throat dazzling me before his greased hand transformed
my body in the baked shed into a salt-slicked block.

Afternoon sun swallowed by his flames. *Righteous desire,*
what he called it—told me god's hand can do as it pleases.

I want to write about roses and lakes, but everything
is slate after that day, a faceless city. Pewter sky hangs

like a cough. No doves left to sing. And no flowers. He
took their petals too. No sound. Muffled Tears. Not even

a shake of cicada wing. After the fire, ash and clouds
morphed to ghosts haunting tracks of my past. The dark

path laid by my father—remnants of dogwood blossoms,
scattered ivory stars on the lawn, my longing to escape.

Father Taunting Her with Psalms

—from Yeats "Leda and the Swan"

She was holding a book in her hand,
being so caught up as she walked
through dead stalks and fresh sod.

It's brute blood of the air, the maples
copper-flame assailing her eyes,
the leaf blower droning in her ears.

There was something bronze in her—
a rage, a knowing, as she lay *in the white rush*
of quiet clouds.

There was no lake,
but *a sudden blow: the great wings beating still*
There was only *a broken wall,*
the burning roof and tower, ash

and brittle leaves swirling *above*
the staggering girl, her thighs caressed.

Dark swallows circled the sky,
a weak wind rustled the trees.

She was dizzy.
And feverish.

Next to the garage tools, he pointed
to a ragged leather-bound KJV Bible.

She put on his knowledge with his power,
"Come now; it's time to read the Psalms."

The Summer the Flashbacks Begin

Blood pools at my ankles,
color of plums. For months,
my arms and legs are needle

numb, muscles weak, pillared
in bed like stone. Fog clouds
my brain. I can't read. Outside,

goldfinches graze in summer
grass. They turn upside down
nibbling begonias, thistle and thorn.

I watch, will myself to live—peaches
help, meaty fruit with enough
sweet to chew. I'm fatigued, afraid

to drive. One time I met a friend
for coffee. You had to carry me
up the stairs when I got home. Now,

I rarely leave our room. You know
something is wrong. You're
terribly worried. On good days

I step out of bed, dress
myself, feed leafy greens
to a doe near the backdoor

hydrangeas. Once, you recorded
my hands doling out
spinach, greeting her dark eyes

and hungry mouth in the haze
of June. You still watch it
on days you need marvel—

her tiptoe out of thicket
towards sustenance—soft joy
in my voice, our flower heads

bowed, unfurling deep blues.

It's comin' up a cloud

my father would say as
        Kentucky storms roiled dark over
        the Ohio River to us. Dahlias

bloomed next to fat zucchinis, tomatoes
        swelled in the garden of sweet berries.
        My toes shone pearls in the grass,

while I scribbled love poems to *Matt B.*, doodled
        in colored pens, looped hearts,
        signed my name *Miss America,*

listened to a Walkman blasting Faith
        Hill's "This Kiss" (snuck from a friend),
        under my foamy headphones. My father fiddled

until the downpour started. Sunflowers gathered
        the last light before the first crack
        of thunder. *Go inside,* he would say. Rock

shards from the rose beds pierced my feet
        on the long trek back. I stood poised
        in our mudroom—my stripped

jumper, pink jelly shoes on the floor,
        as his rough fingers reached
        inside me, as the deluge of rain

        smacked the covered window.

Shapeshifter

—for Kevin

*People come and go
like the weather*
My father used to say

as clouds dispersed
under the breaking |blue
sky. Thunder of nearby

horses shook, and I hated
when he said that |tainting
what was left of chance

joy| I fell asleep cold,
but woke to your whistle
praise of sunken

stalks, husks in the fallow
meadows and dwindling
light| You flew in like a sparrow

from the north, not afraid
to settle in the mahogany
and scarlet leaves that matched

the bruises he left |my shattered
bones of winter. Others winged
to azure waters, believed

his sunny sermons
and prayers, tricked| by fire
and tongues. But you feathered

in the gray and shadows, sheltered
near my window, through all
the harsh weather and stayed.

Supercilious Man Calling Himself Angel

I hated the way his laugh bellowed
as summer breathed its last spray
of color around the hedges
while his wife, sometimes
my mother, folded laundry,
unconcerned with the children
playing, the boys shoving little girls
underneath the bed. It always began
with a polite knock. Mother's TV
muffled his sounds, white noise
and bunny ears. *Did she know?*
Outside, an eerie dampness. Small
birds beginning to flee, navigate
the dark by star.

After Sodom There Was the Cave

Scratch nails on the walls to mark the days, count
the number of times. Look for pale sun to rise, drag
your belly like a snake to the slippery edge where light
pierces swollen eyes. Examine cut skin. Dream of fire.
Dream of burning down what city comes after Sodom.
Listen for bears and bats. Practice Mozart with rocks you
find in the cave. Wonder if you can turn already-dead-bat
bones into a weapon or a stake. Become quiet and small.
Hope sediment of the cave swallows you, folds into the
ground. Pray miners discover dynamite, blow up the cave.
Strategize how best to hide. Practice multiplication tables
in your head. Remember cream camellias. Ask why beauty
exists? Wonder why you couldn't turn to salt like your
mother. See angels holding your hand in the night—
the gold and pearl bracelet jingling from your small wrist,
sliding up and down.

You Asked Me About My Mother

Once, my sister and I found lost
ducklings in the hedgerows

around our small house. My father
drove them to the river, his hands

steady on the steering wheel
of his old truck as they chirped

in the shoebox—he placed each one
gently in the riverbed, told us

their mother was never coming back
as he set them loose in the cold water,

barely enough feathers to preen, trees
still shaking off rain from last night's storm.

I Dream of the Orca Carrying Her Dead Calf for 17 Days

A Pacific Northwest orca likely bonded closely with her calf before it died, which could help explain her record-breaking emotional sojourn.
—National Geographic

Seventeen days of extra weight
on her back. Starts and stop
of shallow breath. Muscle needed

to carry her daughter through
torrents of deep currents. Stars flicker
in the empty nights. Her young

calf, stiff and cold, the heaviness
lingers. Reluctant mornings she wakes
to blurry sun. Boats circle near

the coastline, wisteria and salt hang
in the air by the dirty city. Gulls swoop
above tangled plastic and seaweed, dart

into waves, ready to bite at death.
At high tide she wants to disappear
below the frigid cresting, swim away

into thick dark kelp until she finds
her way back to a deep living well
of surrender—instead she treads

for miles, the arid heaving in her chest,
instead of a mother who casually averted
her eyes each time the door clasped shut,

each time
        a small death.

Love Poem for the Year After My Hip Surgery

—for J, S & E

1. Winter

You push me in the cranky wheelchair,
each bump hurts my hip and pride,
so I stare at the pavement glitter

to distract from my pain. I'm not
speaking much these days,
stomach raw from the months

of Tramadol and peanut butter
crackers. I resent my shower
chair, and the times I need you

to help me dress. My breath haloes
you in the cold—geese honk, break
the silence over the icy pond.

2. Spring

I should be walking by now, but
I'm not. Eager redbuds blaze against
the slate sky of March as I limp

to the car, drive to rehab. Shy
others, buds ready to unfurl,
persist. After another rough

session, a luna moth flies near
the edge of our lined trees—ambles
above the bramble canopy.

3. Summer

Few under thirty can bear
to watch a young body
suffer. So, we learn to wade

alone, except those friends
that brought balloons and baked
ziti. Sometimes, you grumble

as I steady in the sparkling pool—
gravity's invisible weight pushes
against my tired legs as I learn

to walk again, find footing.

4. Fall

By September, the fawns have grown
sturdy, and camellias have tender buds
again, those late blooms of the South.

I practice walking without crutches,
sit beneath sugar maples, a burst
of leaves until I am fire-soaked

in passion. I come back to marriage
and sex, to red-tinged camellias; come
back to my dogs, and apples—

the boldly fallen.

Lot's Nameless Wife Takes Inventory

—after C.T. Salazar

rabbit	foot	fox	paw	robin
egg	blue	birds	fly	-ing
ash	sky	grass	hopper	sp-
arrows	dart	to	flee	flamed
city	swirls	of	smoke	pin
green	lace	wings	burn	earth-
worms	snow	-y owls	bruise	blue
whales	starve	in	melting	sea
otters	whirl	rain	bows:of	oil
covers	crows	pecking	my	salt

My Thoughts as I Look Back

When I see flame of sun washing over these hurting days
I turn immobile, wonder why anyone would want to look?

There, we grew raspberries and knew the splendor of June,
day hung like a loose sundress off the shoulders, night a snug

cardigan. When we moved back to this place, I waited
for you, birds in the tall grass near the pond with cream

lily pads. I painted a small house for their feathered young,
hung it on the crape myrtles, but it's rain-spattered

and empty. Our omens came in warm winters, whispers
of frost in late May, and heaps of dead bees—wings

shimmering like angels in searing heat. We zoomed. Paid
less attention to what mattered, love and springtime:

How the cherry trees let go, snow blush
blossoms after they finish weeping.

Birthday Elegy

*

I walk back from the pelican bay,
sand stuck to the cold spaces
between my curled toes as I press
them against the tile, tap
your shoulder. You're groggy,
but lean in to kiss me—you taste
of bourbon and cherry bitters
from last night, caterpillar
eyebrows messy from the pillow.
You whisper *happy birthday
gorgeous,* ask to go down on me.
I pull down the satin over my legs,
welcome your tongue—
I don't have the courage yet
to tell you that your father passed
away in the still-dark morning,
my phone pulsing as I come.
My brain cannot process zippy
happy birthday texts aside the funeral
arrangements. I let you hold me
longer than I should.

**

At breakfast we eat cold eggs in silence.

Faint coast and gulls fade out
of the mirror as I drive.

Rain starts to fall, then heavier,
thick clouds follow us home.

You write the eulogy. Back
at home, you give me

an antique piano music box
that plays Rachmaninoff. It spins

a melody into the corners
of our somber room. I crank

the turnkey to hear notes
sooth over the bleat of this day—

your scour for trashed treasures—
sorrow opens a new decade,

my thirtieth birthday, prelude
to your steadfast love,

a grinding song.

A Queen Resurfaces

I remember the first time her barb
pierced my wrist, a yellow jacket
away from the hive, shimmering
wings and sleek, ordered body—

venom blasted through my hand,
stole my breath, crepe myrtles hung
in my blurred vision. The unexpected
sharp pain and chaos as I chased

a loose ball near the hidden,
buried nest. Let me warn you,
her sting said. Some messengers burst
in with needed aggression. Take

your pen as my stinger and write
it all down. Remember the last days
of summer fading away, his prim
dahlias and secret tequila. The small

girl with roped daisies braiding
her hair, his musky cologne and lips
pressed on her neck, shadows of him
lingering in the cold shower, water

beading at her feet, bone-white
and shimmer soaked. These memories
swarm, and the ground is warming.
But I'm older now, ready and willing to sting.

Spring Collection

I feel her spirit
quivering in the dogwood
full of blossoms, a pink-lit tree
in the cool, gray tug of May.

My mother said beauty is only skin deep.
It's like the horizon, it goes on
forever, but you can't touch it.

Therefore, I'm invisible,
and try to crawl out of my skin.

I drape myself in fabric, tiny chandeliers, paint
my lips velvet. I try to become
a catalog she refuses to bless.

She has become a ghost
in every form a shadow can take.
Rain calls her back, rusty pails
of marigolds and rubber boots.

There she is circling the river, an otter coat.
There she is diffusing air, perfume on a scarf.

The swan circles the pond, nuzzles her cygnets,
sun spreads honey on their feathers.

A Word She Taught Me Called Pleasure

My mother wanted so much for
the maples to flame, and the air
to brisk as we walked through
the apple orchard, filling our baskets
with the ripe and heavy fruit—katydids
and a few songbirds left on the branches
before the silence. She wanted everything
to be golden and fleeting, spark and awe.

I wanted the slip of dark to be removed,
her happy under the summer afghan
surrounded by sunflowers and violets
while her warm and present hands
braided my hair—blueberry muffins
and zucchini bread in the kitchen,
and the sky the color of her eyes,
calm and unequivocal again
after all the rain.

October

—after Linda Pastan

How suddenly the
dark drop of autumn begins.
The sky dims to plum

and shadow. I feel
like Eurydice walking
away with my feet

stinging, the music
fading, overtaken by
Hades' sharp venom.

Equanimity

Log into *insight timer* twice a day. Ask
    for swan calm circling
        the clear lake. River otter
            laps as dusk hangs tufts of clouds,

bridal lace. A friend posts, "Legally in Love!"
    and my fingertip wands
        a small heart, internet
            magic spreads valentine

red. My aunt obsessed with Elvis,
    one who calls me Nikki, my favorite
        nickname, who's survived on
            Coke and Zoloft since her rich

husband died twenty years ago,
    may get out of bed, hot-roller
        her hair, and put her dentures in
            to see Austin Butler sinfully shake his hips.

Hanging baskets with American flags
    filled with orange marigolds, small flames on a day
        Roe v. Wade is overturned, but my body
            climbed to rhododendrons and waterfalls.

Someone gave me a tiny spoon with strawberry
    ice-cream as I catwalked down Main St.
        with rose sugar and rosemary herbs
            for my sweetheart who chefs for me . . .

And my yoga teacher with M.S. (who knows
    I tested negative but still have symptoms)
        ends every class with "the light & beauty in me
            sees and honors the light & beauty in you."

Castle Elementary in Southern Indiana Asks Its Third Graders to Sell Earth Day T-Shirts

I sold only one tie-dyed globe shirt
in the maze of cornfields, on a street
papered with my father's salvation leaflets.
But from trees came breath and shade, anchor
for a quiet girl in nature who turned toward joy
of birches sloughing off, confetti of dogwoods
eyeleting the lawn. April gods—swarms
of ladybugs, and doves, blue-eyed grass
under the vast midwestern sky.
My mission? To save trees instead of souls,
tangible love of leaf and bark I held
under my small fingers, grasped
that I belong here on earth.

Prayer

I walk in silence among clover and miss you.
Evening light drips honey over the grass,
my naked feet. Above the rapture of birds
and slipping blue, clouds absorb the vespers.
The next day petitions fall from the sky, rain.
It seems like nothing hears us—this longing
everywhere. We live somewhere between
promises—like dashes, small connectors
of words. I search for you. Link together
signs. Sugar peas and red tulips, whispers
of you. How easily I'm mistaken. I pray
in lyric, insist verses open parachutes
for the heart, tumble into a soft landing—
what other rhythm do I know?

Horses & Roses

I work with what I'm given—
a herd of rescued horses, grazing
in the summer wind.

Mulch and labor, tying ropes eases
the burden of the unspoken,
heat and sweat.

Later, a friend knocks on the door sharing
good fortune, and I cherish those

who fill my empty bowl. Some days
the thorns are less prominent, the pain dull.
It's a tough hide to the bee sting.

These are the days where I don't push as hard.
Others, I allow myself to rest for hours.

I soften like the mustangs—someone gentle
brushes my hair, runs their tender hands
through the course tangles.

Not even the swarming flies biting my calves
can disturb my peace.

Lost to the pasture and wild roses,
I lie down in the afternoon sun and sleep.

Coda

I play the piano gently to forget him.
This is how the heart makes a coda of
terror and grief. Evening light tassels
the sky while broken chords drift
in the room, diminish. The notes
puncture silence, my wrist hovers
like a crane to strike the next key.
This song is familiar, but not yet
spoken. My father, the first man I loved
only wanted to hurt me. Now, I reach
under the hollow of my bone to hear
harmony—the embrace of you, soft
mornings that grace my days. At night,
my tea steams to the glow of fireflies.
We play cards, and laugh, kiss goodnight.
To forget him I play the piano gently.

Thanksgiving Psalm

We stir in silence, a meditation of dishes
as the moon shines and exhales over the stove.
The apricots glow little fires on our plates.
Here in this kitchen, there is no war. No Father
we wage allegiance to. When I was a child,
my father read Psalms that praised violence
in the name of his God, then promised feasts
and bounties. *Give thanks,* he said. *Bow your heads.*
A misplaced laugh or wrong look, a clanking knife
as he prayed? I shuddered when his fists hit the table.
Praise my insolent blade today. No scriptures,
only clean slices of figs and brie. Praise warm
cider and gin. Praise the silk cheesecake under
my tongue. Praise quiet, the willows and wind.

Early Mornings with My Father

Snow falls in late December, weak coffee
brews, and I am back in our yellow kitchen,
porch lights frame shadows around icicles.

I wipe the sleep from my eyes, tiptoe
the mauve carpet like a fawn,
join my father at the oval oak table.

It is quiet, all but the sigh and drip
of the Mr. Coffee before the sun peaks
rosy over the coalmines and cornfields.

A cardinal rests on the feeder outside
the frosted window, gentle gift to us both,
syncopated space of our union. I am here

to hug him goodbye before the woe
of his day settles like permafrost,
muffled weather radio voices rumble.

Before the grit and grease of steel boilers
stain the stitched shirt he wears resigned,
Alcoa's emblem tucked under flannel.

I learn to love silence and darkness here,
slow sips of bittersweet grace notes,
rest of a measured morning in a mug.

Outside, the engine of his brown truck pings,
he lifts each boot like a cement brick,
laces drawn like a harpist pulling strings.

My early rising an attempt to sit with him,
ease the pain of years of a job he hates
while the day is still kind to us both.

Christmas Eve

I hope we'll drink whiskey with friends
and laugh until we're annoying
each other with bad dancing and jokes,
singing carols and Joni Mitchell's *River*
at the upright piano. I hope we're snuggling
in our navy blanket that weighs more
than our skittery dog, and a fire crackles.
I hope we watch *It's a Wonderful Life*
and feel Jimmy Stewart's swollen lip,
taste our own blood, sorrow while
the tree sparkles, shadows brighten.
I hope we bake cinnamon rolls
and eat too many. Complain about
glitter on the packages—I hope we still
love each other enough to fuss
about the small things—mice on
the stove, ants marching in our shower.
I hope the moon keeps us awake
a little longer than usual, and you slip
a secret, slide my hair behind
the curl of my ear, and we make love.
Then, I'll fall asleep knowing the dark
of winter settling in my bones
as we dream again.

He Asks Me Why I Love Winter

in the middle of February, camellias
bursting over the lawn,

      kissing the ground
      with their NARS lips. Because it's the best

of Vivaldi's seasons, the violin pulsing
up the spine, *allegro*'s frostbite

      shivers, then slows to the static
          of the record needle, reminds me

            of snow and us
                in the hot shower.

Afterward, curled together in a heap
      of sherpa. The cool palettes

          of blue and gray thrum
      at *largo*. It's easier to see

in the pale gold morning, the parade
      of robins that have gritted

through the harsh, their nests
      kept cozy for the turquoise

      eggs to come. Buds that drop
pearls on a pear tree near the park. I get to taste

bittersweet—grapefruit and chicory,
      cardamom tea biting

at me in the dark hours
       of waking. Root magic scattered

along the cold creek.

After Talking to Poet Chen Chen About Teaching a Class on Happy Poems

Everything I thought was missing
is here when spring accepts
an invitation from an unlikely friend,

and the tulips have pushed their way
towards the lavish sun from whatever
darkness regarded them, and you

hold me today in the warm bowl
of morning as we move again towards
light brimming like broth while the days

insist on getting brighter, longer.
I can still hear the owl that lives
somewhere behind the engorged

camellias, and I get raptured strolling
by the magnolia after last night's rain,
knowing now that some favor slow

starts. I used to think that memory
would shake me bare into a winter
that would never leave. What cold

did I believe would always be with me?
Today everything has decided to live
again, greening and expanding,

blooming against whatever unkind cut
was made, to go all in from blade
and root, insisting on its own joy.

The Nestling Near Your Magnolia Tree

—for Ron Maple

I worried for days that the cat
who slinks our small street got to her first.
I want to believe she made it—that her feathers
have grown rich cerulean, a winged mercy
about to flit from the branch into the gardenia
bush next door. And, I could point to her
in the thick green leaves along the peonies
in full bloom and bluster, with a kind smile
like you, when all you said was, *you did*
the right thing after I told you that I found her
shivering on the sidewalk, afraid to touch her,
only covering her open mouth and frail body
with a dropped leaf. Now absence settles in spring
as I walk by your house and empty swing.

Ambivalent Selkie Finds Joy

I preferred depths where sunlight cannot reach.
Comfortable in bedrock and silt. I needed time
for my seal-eyes to adjust to the burn of sunset.
Weak legs and ocean ears. I missed moonlight
reflected on the dark water, my own loneliness.
You waited for me to hear the echo of summer
birds waking in the morning instead of the bleak
numb. Now, I slip in on my robe as bees hug
clover for honey, and the dog nestles in my lap.
We eat strawberry jam on toast, lick soft butter
from our fingers. We place empty dishes in the sink,
wipe away grit and stain. Some memories wash up
dead coral, broken glass. But, I'm sturdy now.
I've grown feet and spine. We walk the shoreline,
find magnificent shells. My toes curl into the sand.
I think I'll keep this skin.

Summer Communion

A Sunday walk in August, cicadas shaking
& crepe myrtles snowing petals. I come across
disposed of tree branches, someone else's garbage,
lined-up elephant ears drooping
on the eaves of the street.
What compels me to stop, trace
my fingers over the rivered veins?
Breaking one off for a keepsake is a struggle,
but I wriggle it away.
The house owner catches me & grins,
knows I've found a secret treasure, a blessing I'm taking
home with me. I don't care that I'm caught.
How good it feels not to be self-conscious,
a light breeze unable to nudge my sweaty hair.
I tuck the leaf in my pocket, & spend a few hours
writing at my desk. At dinner, I marvel
at how briefly summer gets to be this sweet
sipping peach wine, shimmering
in the sun. I'm done with sacraments, a broken
body & blood. I chew cheddar biscuits & green
beans. Later, I loosen my dress strap & a man kisses
my bare shoulder as the fan spins cool air.

Update on Lot's Wife

—after Mary Szybist

Are you sure she has two daughters like the Bible says?
Balloon arches, Bach and bubbles make her happy—Also,
Carolina wrens teakettle the wooded path in autumn. She
delights in piano, which ear-lined her to hear minor harmonies.
Envy occasionally hijacks her days, zaps an electric light. Finds
friends disappear after they have babies, or the men marry.
Genesis was never her origin story, left too many questions. His
honey coffee blend, kiss wake her most mornings. Presence buds
insight, which sometimes blooms sound. Judy Garland movies.
Jogging clears her mind when ghosts shake her bed. So does,
kombucha and Lululemon, which she spends too much on.
Lindt truffles melt moods. Lavender calms. Lot's jawline.
Monarch butterflies disappearing—mostly climate change,
neglect worries her. Often, she remembers she was given
over to angels far too young. It stirs her; wakes her. Often,
piano taught her to sit in silent darkness, become a song.
Qigong helped her walk when her legs were needle-numb.
Red shades of lipstick. Dior Rogue. Sequins of sew-joy,
streetlights goldening spring rain. Swift, Taylor. Tinsel hair.
Tina, who was kind to her, then died of ovarian cancer. Lace
underwear—watching bedazzled supermodels stomp a catwalk,
Victoria's Secret Fashion show, even though she hid this. Orca
whales, and friends she misses the most, show up in her dreams.
Xenon lights illuminated her bent hip that needed crutches. Loves
yellow, her grandmother's favorite color of rose. She searches
Zillow when distracted, could probably write more poems.

I Imagine Being a Worm

In the dark of earth
without the burden of seeing
or hearing him. Dew-soaked
in dirt's kind hold, burrowed
safely into a ball, marbled
like a peony before it blooms,
blocking his intruding fingers
I wriggle through silt and stone,
regenerate, circulate new blood
to the parts he severed—
an iron soul determined to survive,
sifting, crawling in decomposed
bones, no longer afraid
of what I find, feast on.

Resentment

—after "Garden Song" by Phoebe Bridgers

I know that song well, but it's getting softer.
My fisted lungs no longer clutch, but hum
an echo in distant hills where I climb to moss
and waterfall that cool my chest, dowse

my hair draped over my shoulder knob that used
to always ache. The days no longer feel like a burden
or a dream. Swans bicker & float over a lake,
skimming gnats. I paddle down a mud-slaked river

alive as my veins—ospreys dive for minnows
that are lucky to live a few years. I can sleep again.
I'm not afraid to wake up, see you and flecks of dust
when my eyes open. It's like slicing skin off fruit.

I pray, cut peaches for my oatmeal in the morning,
watch clouds turn to roses in the blue of evening.

Duplex for the Waiting

A friend reminds me your name means beloved.
You must hear mercy in the birdsong and breeze.

> I hear mercy in the birdsong and June breeze.
> What guilt drives you to silence and distance?

Guilt drives us to silence and repentance.
I want to tell you I know why songs are shy.

> Ask me why some songs are shy, and I'll say,
> remember the solace of the shaded trees.

Let's sit beneath the solace of shadow. Here:
the peaches are ready now, ripe and sweet.

> The peaches are ready now, ripe and sweet
> in the park where I write poems that wait.

I write poems that wait, forgive the seasons.
A friend reminds me your name means beloved.

Andante

It is like the moment the deer decides to eat from your hand, then follows the trail deep into the woods, but there is only a narrow gap in the thicket and bramble, and the leaves grow so dense, so green, that the deer vanishes, and you can't see anything as the heat crescendos then lilts into a dry silence, and then suddenly it's January, and light streaks a blue vein across the winter sky, and a flock of geese flap over a lake, you hear the wingbeat, the shoreline pebbles trembling, and start walking.

Broken Chords

Spring and forsythia in dusk's somber
        air as my fingers tease Chopin's *Nocturne,* play
andante. Scraggy shadows frame your jawline

as you stir sauce into a recipe, milkweeds sidle
        up the once-white-picket fence, shed shines
lassiez-faire in the yawning sun. We began

as teenagers exploring our bodies, staring hours
        at glow-stars on your bedroom ceiling. I traced
you. My fingers and lips. It's muscle memory

now. The arpeggios sound beautiful, broken
        notes drift in the room. Minor key lulls
darkly over life's tumult. Nothing new to say

about the day, only mosquitos warm-blood need
        to swat away. Cloudless blue and the unspoken
between us. Dimming light glimmers past

the window. The piece ends, resolves. Grief finds
        a major key as the chords turn bright, ascending.
You kiss my neck, say dinner is ready.

Legacy

His friends called him *Groove* before
he found mean Jesus, and he still
played the guitar. In one picture,
he's smiling before his mother died.
He was only five when she withered
to a sparrow, and the angel of death
shook the window open and left him
her bones—before his Pap had a nervous
breakdown, and he went to foster care.
Before the broken chords, I remember
the first time my small hands poked
him a song on our old Wurlitzer.
He was proud of me. Before
I knew words or poetry, I had a song
under my fingers. When people ask me
what he gave me, I tell them the blues
of my eyes & angles of my cheekbones,
but mostly I tell them the music.

Notes

Several of the persona poems in this collection originate from the Genesis account of Lot and his wife. The story is recounted in Genesis 19: 1–38. Lot, his wife and two daughters were visited by two angels who urged them to flee the city of Sodom before its imminent destruction by God.

As they fled, Lot's wife disobeyed the angels' command to not look back; and therefore, as a punishment to her disobedience, was turned into a pillar of salt. The angels give Lot permission to flee to the nearby town of Zoar but being overtaken by fear, he takes his daughters into the nearby mountains, and they live together in a cave.

I used the story as a backdrop to frame the harsh religious ideology that I encountered in my childhood with hopes to subvert the refrain of all of patriarchy which is designed to denigrate women, marginalized people and the earth.

"Aftermath": is an ekphrastic poem based on the abstract painting *Lot's Wife* by artist Anselm Kiefer which is currently displayed at the Cleveland Museum of Art.

"Father Taunting Her with Psalms": The italics in the poem are lines or phrases taken from the Yeats poem "Leda and the Swan." The selected text emphasizes the parallels between the adolescent girl in the poem and Leda.

"I Dream of the Orca Carrying Her Dead Calf for 17 Days": is taken from a National Geographic article which states, "an orca whale has finally dropped her dead calf, which she'd been pushing with her head for at least 17 days and 1,000 miles off the Pacific Northwest coast, in an unprecedented show of mourning that drew international attention." Cuthbert, Lori, and Douglas Main. "Orca

Mother Drops Calf, After Unprecedented 17 Days of Mourning." National Geographic, nationalgeographic.com/animals/article/orca-mourning-calf-killer-whale-northwest-news. Accessed 1 Dec. 2024.

"Lot's Nameless Wife Takes Inventory": This poem is written after the poem "Noah's Nameless Wife Takes Inventory" by poet C.T. Salazar which addresses themes of climate change with another nameless female mentioned in the book of Genesis.

"Thanksgiving Psalm": There are at least 22 notable imprecatory psalms in the biblical Book of Psalms which praise violence.

"Horses & Roses": This poem was written about my time spent doing equine therapy at Mending Strides Ranch in Mint Hill, NC which has helped many survivors. I have fond memories with Maria, the trainer and founder of the organization, and her beautiful rescued mustangs.

"Coda": Coda is a musical term that signifies the concluding passage of a piece or movement.

"Andante": Andante is a musical term that means moderately slow or at a "walking pace."

About the Author

Brooke Lehmann's poems have been featured in *Poet Lore, Tar River Poetry, Pedestal Magazine,* and others. She was longlisted for the 2022 *Palette Poetry* Sappho Prize for Women Poets, and her chapbook manuscript, *Pillar of Exquisite Sorrows,* was named a finalist in *Tusculum Review's* 2023 Chapbook Prize. Her poem "Thanksgiving Psalm" was awarded first place in the 2024 Charles Edward Eaton contest for *Pinesong.* Brooke holds a B.S. from Purdue University and is an Arts and Science Council Cultural Leadership Training program graduate. She serves as Poet-In-Residence for Charlotte Center for Mindfulness.

www.ingramcontent.com/pod-product-compliance
Lightning Source LLC
Chambersburg PA
CBHW030912170426
43193CB00009BA/825